THE TEN
TESTAMENTS

THE TEN
TESTAMENTS

LESSONS FROM THE GREATEST TEACHER OF ALL TIME

SCOTT CAMPBELL

WINEPRESS WP PUBLISHING

WinePress Publishing (PO Box 428, Enumclaw, WA 98022) functions only as book publisher. As such, the ultimate design, content, editorial accuracy, and views expressed or implied in this work are those of the author.

All Scripture quotations, unless otherwise indicated, are taken from the *Holy Bible: New International Version*®. *NIV*®. Copyright © 1973, 1978, 1984 by International Bible Society. Used by permission of Zondervan. All rights reserved.

ISBN 13: 978-1-57921-954-3
ISBN 10: 1-57921-954-3
Library of Congress Catalog Card Number: 2008921225

To my mother,
who taught our family these lessons
through her example and her unselfish love.

As the Father has sent me,
I am sending you.
John 20:21

Go into all the world and preach the
good news to all creation.
Mark 16:15

CONTENTS

ACKNOWLEDGMENTS

I would like to thank Tom and Julie Brucato, Sister Delouise Menges, Sister Teresa Mitchell, and Robin Madden for their generous contribution to this book. They played a significant role in clarifying the vision of *The Ten Testaments*.

A special thanks to Ric Hopkins, Lydia Penaranda, Pat Dowler, Caroline Welsh, Denise Daggett, Debbie Stephens, Scott Lange, and Denny Krause for their assistance in the production of the audio book. Without their help, this project would not have been possible.

A very special thanks to my wonderful wife and two beautiful daughters for their love and patience during this journey. May we continue to live this life of love together.

I thank Jesus, who humbles and inspires me every day with His guidance and blessings.

CHAPTER 1

LOVE

A long time ago, by the shore of Galilee, in the prosperous fishing village of Capernaum, a crowd gathered to listen to a dynamic new teacher. Great excitement grew among the people because the teacher taught with great authority about an exciting new way to live.

The fishing community responded favorably to the teacher and he became very popular; however, the political leaders adapted slowly to His way of thinking.

A lawyer made his way through the crowd because he wanted to test the teacher. The lawyer asked, "Teacher, which is the greatest commandment in the Law?"

The teacher replied, "Love the Lord your God with all your heart and with all your soul and with your entire mind. This is the first and greatest commandment. And the second commandment is similar."

The crowd gathered closer to listen with great interest . . .

A new commandment I give you:
Love one another.
As I have loved you,
so you must love one another.
All men will know that you are my disciples
if you love one another.
John 13:34–35

TESTAMENT I

I WILL LOVE MY NEIGHBOR

Since the beginning of time, people have searched for the key to happiness. *To love my neighbor* is the key to happiness.

Who is my neighbor?
- My neighbor includes all people, because everyone is a child of God.
- My neighbor is anyone whom I have the opportunity to serve at any given moment.
- My neighbor is the man or woman I see walking on the street or shopping in the market.
- My neighbor is a fellow worker, a teammate, or a customer.
- My neighbor is my sister, my brother, my mother, and my father.
- My neighbor is a close friend as well as my enemy.
- My neighbor is the homeless, the elderly, and the sick.
- My neighbor is anyone to whom I can offer a smile, a gesture of politeness, or a greeting of "hello."

Because everyone is equal in God's eyes, I will love all of God's people. I will treat all men and women like members of my own family. I will praise all children so they will feel important, and I will love and respect the elderly, as well as the mentally and physically challenged.

I will love my neighbor.

I will treat my neighbor in the manner I desire to be treated. I will employ the "Golden Rule" to convert a neighbor into a friend. I will carefully select the thoughts, words, and actions I send toward my neighbor, knowing he or she will most likely

Do to others
as you would have them do to you.
Luke 6:31

return them to me. If I send love, my neighbor will return love. If I send anger, my neighbor will return anger. If I send generosity, my neighbor will return generosity. No matter what expression I send, I will choose an expression of love.

I will love my neighbor.

I will not allow a day to pass when I haven't made an attempt to befriend at least one person. I have the opportunity to send a message of love to every person I meet. Because love must be created, I will make an effort to begin a conversation, to share a kind gesture, or to perform a good deed. When I meet a new acquaintance, I realize that the opportunity to begin a friendship is here and now, because we may never cross paths again.

I will love my neighbor.

I will not rely on first impressions when I meet a new acquaintance and I will not judge an individual based on appearance, race, sex, or religion. Nor will I judge an individual based on wealth, education, or possessions. I will celebrate the fact that everyone is created equal, but different. I will not judge anyone, because I realize that my neighbors are at different maturity levels and we all are subject to many different circumstances. Therefore, I intend to share love with everyone I meet.

I have the opportunity to love and serve my neighbor in many ways:

- I will use my arms to reach out to strangers.
- I will use my feet to visit the sick.
- I will use my hands to pick up those who have fallen.
- I will use my ears to listen to the downhearted.
- I will use my voice to encourage the weak.
- I will use my heart to love my neighbor.

I will love God, my Creator, most of all. God created human beings in His image. God *is* love, and He is the source of all

Love your enemies and pray
for those who persecute you,
that you may be sons
of your Father in heaven.
Matthew 5:44–45

love. God loves me and I vow to spread His love to everyone I meet. He knows what is in my heart. I will radiate His love by serving the needs of others. I am not ashamed to serve others, because when I do, I know I am serving God.

I will make an extra effort to share love with those considered to be my enemies. I find it easy to love those who love me; however, it's not as easy to love those who do not love me, those who hurt me, or those who slander me. I know that love has the power to convert an enemy into a friend. If someone ignores me, I will smile and say, "Hello." If someone injures me, I will turn my cheek and be willing to receive additional abuse. If people slander me, I will avoid the temptation to gossip about them with my tongue. I will use the contagious power of love to warm the hearts of others.

- I will smile at those who frown.
- I will wave at those who step in front of me.
- I will extend a handshake to those who do not welcome me.
- I will love my neighbor.

I will not permit a natural or synthetic barrier to separate me from my neighbor. However, I am determined to go out of my way to visit a neighbor in order to show love and kindness. I will build bridges over obstacles and clear paths through politics in order to show love toward my neighbor.

I will love my neighbor.

There is one prerequisite to loving my neighbor: I must love myself so that I can give love to others. If I love myself, I find it easier to attract love into my life. And when I love myself, I am filled with the kind of love God gives me to share with others. Since I must love my neighbor as I love myself, I must first love myself.

Love your neighbor as yourself.
Matthew 22:39

The greatest act of love is to lay down one's life for a neighbor. If I see a neighbor in a life-threatening situation, I will offer assistance, within reason, hoping my neighbor would do the same for me.

Love creates an atmosphere of sharing and helping. It brings people closer so we can work in harmony toward a common goal rather than compete in an environment promoting winning and losing.

Love is the greatest form of communication. It makes people happy and strengthens relationships with trust and respect. Love brings people closer so that life becomes more meaningful.

I will use the power of love whenever I come in contact with another human being.

I will love my neighbor.

CHAPTER 2

FORGIVENESS

The following day, a local tax collector invited the teacher to his home to dine with other tax collectors. The tax collectors were known to eat and drink in excess, as well as participate in unlawful behavior, such as taking advantage of the poor and uneducated.

As the teacher shared a meal with the tax collectors, He told them stories to illustrate love and forgiveness. When the evening came to an end, many of the tax collectors had acquired great respect and admiration for this new teacher.

The following day, a political leader asked the teacher why He associated with people who indulged in reckless living. The teacher knew the town's inhabitants would judge Him because of His association with such people. He replied to the political leader and said that His purpose was not to serve the healthy, but the sick. He then began to address the crowd . . .

I have not come to call the righteous,
but sinners to repentance.
Luke 5:32

TESTAMENT II

I WILL FORGIVE MY NEIGHBOR

Creating relationships is necessary for a successful life. The relationships I form allow me to function in a world where everyone depends on each other. Relationships are built with love and trust—similar to the way a rosebush thrives with water and sunlight. Nurture and tender loving care must be given to both. When people experience harm to their relationships (anything from a simple misunderstanding to a hurtful verbal attack), it's as if a drought or darkness stunts the growth. As a result, the relationship becomes damaged and the healing power of forgiveness becomes necessary in order to restore the relationship to the point where they can love and trust one another again.

I will practice forgiveness.

I find it difficult to communicate with someone whom I have injured until I apologize and ask for forgiveness. My guilty conscience prompts me to convey my sorrow and remorse to the other person as soon as possible. To postpone an apology may result in ill-feelings and resentment toward each other. I will courageously approach my neighbor and say the words, "I am sorry; please forgive me. I made a mistake, and I promise not to allow it to happen again. What can I do to make it right?" I hope that my neighbor will understand that I value our relationship and will forgive me for my offense.

Forgiveness is a two-way street. The relationship with my neighbor can be saved only if there is a mutual desire to restore the relationship. Both parties must participate in the forgiveness process. My apology and my neighbor's acceptance of the apology must mutually occur in order for the healing power of forgiveness to be effective.

Likewise, if my neighbor offends me and asks for my forgiveness, I will forgive him or her as soon as possible. I will treat my

Be merciful,
just as your Father is merciful.
Luke 6:36

neighbor the same way I like to be treated. This is love. This is forgiveness.

I will practice forgiveness.

Occasionally, I must search my heart to see if I have resentful feelings toward anyone. If I have any feelings of anger or revenge, then I probably haven't forgiven a trespass that occurred in the past. Something that my neighbor did or said is still causing me to feel angry or resentful. I must forgive this person as soon as possible in order to restore the healthy and loving attitude God would have me to possess. This act of forgiveness clears my conscience of any regret and restores my inner peace.

Likewise, if I have offended anyone in the past and have not yet asked for forgiveness, I will seek out that individual to ask for forgiveness. There is no need to move forward knowing someone is hurt or angry about something I did or said in the past. He or she is probably waiting for my long-overdue apology.

To commit an offense against my neighbor is also to commit an offense against God. I must ask both my neighbor and my God to forgive me. God gives us all access to Him, and I know He will forgive me when I reach out to Him. God is the source of my strength, and He holds the ultimate power to forgive me when I commit an offense or a wrongdoing. God's forgiveness and healing power give me the strength to find a way to live in harmony with my neighbor. After all, God's forgiveness allows a wrongdoer to be saved, not condemned.

The process of asking God for forgiveness restores my relationship with Him. If I do not ask God for forgiveness, then I'm denying His presence in my life. God loves me so much; He is willing to forgive me. He gives me another chance to discover His grace and divine love. To ask God for forgiveness communicates that I love Him and want to restore His grace in my life. I am saying to God, "I love You. I'm sorry. Please forgive me."

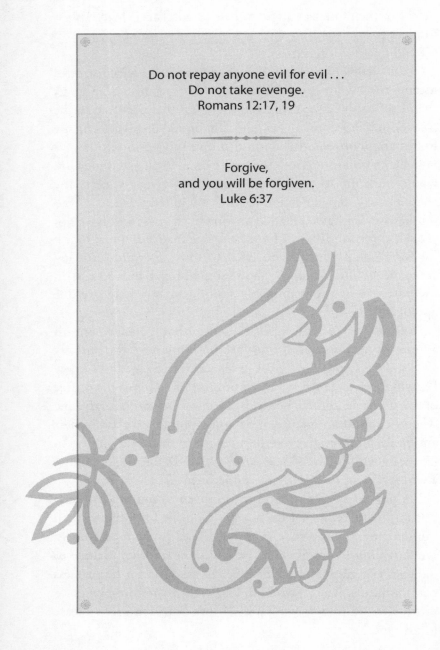

Do not repay anyone evil for evil . . .
Do not take revenge.
Romans 12:17, 19

Forgive,
and you will be forgiven.
Luke 6:37

After God and my neighbor forgive me, then I can forgive myself. When I forgive myself and know that God has restored His grace within me, it becomes easier to move forward with a clear conscience. I can now enjoy a healthy relationship with God, my neighbor, and myself.

I will practice forgiveness.

Forgiveness plays an important role in keeping people happy. When a husband and wife learn to forgive each other, it's easier to enjoy a long and prosperous marriage. A dispute or a quarrel in a marital relationship becomes an opportunity for both parties to forgive each other and learn from their mistakes. When both husband and wife learn to forgive, they develop a better understanding of each other as well as a stronger relationship.

Everyone at one time or another can use the healing power of forgiveness to restore love and trust in a relationship. When I am involved in a relationship where discord exists, I will use the power of forgiveness to mend the relationship as soon as possible.

I will practice forgiveness.

CHAPTER 3

HUMILITY

A few days later, a well-known politician invited the teacher and other distinguished guests to his home for dinner. The homeowner's servant had prepared a large table of veal, roasted corn, raisins, bread, and wine.

As they removed the hot bread from the hearth, many of the guests argued about who would sit in the prestigious position next to the guest of honor. Most everyone wanted to be seated at the head table and to be recognized as a person of importance and high status.

The teacher took His seat and said it did not matter where each person sat. He said they should be willing to sit at the foot of the table, and that it was up to the host to ask the guest to move to a more important position.

The teacher invited everyone to sit down as He spoke on the subject of humility . . .

For everyone who exalts himself
will be humbled,
and he who humbles
himself will be exalted.
Luke 14:11

TESTAMENT III

I WILL BE HUMBLE

I was born into this world as a weak and fragile infant. From the moment of conception, I depended on someone else to provide me with the necessities of life. Later, I matured and became eager to face the world as an independent person thinking I no longer needed help. However, I quickly discovered I could not succeed alone and realized I needed to humbly ask others for help and guidance.

Humility allows me to better handle life's challenges and to more effectively serve others.

I will be humble.

Life is filled with obstacles and adversity. Problems, difficulties, and setbacks often frustrate my efforts. My reaction toward these frustrations will determine how successful I become. The person with very little or no faith will respond with remarks such as "I can't," "That's too difficult," or "That can't be done." However, the humble person who has faith will respond with remarks such as, "If I can't do it alone, I will find someone to help. I have a much greater chance to succeed if someone helps me." If I try to overcome the challenges of life alone, I will often struggle or be defeated. However, with the help of a neighbor, I will experience the love and power that two or more people create when we work together toward a common goal. Therefore, I will set my ego aside and ask my neighbor for help.

The purpose of trials and humiliation is to remind me that I am a weak and vulnerable child of God. Since my life is really in God's hands, I need His help and guidance. God provides answers to those who seek Him. I need only to consult Him on a regular basis. The truly humble will seek God.

To be humble means to tolerate adversity with patience. I will overcome the troubles of life with the help of God and

Do nothing out of selfish ambition
or vain conceit, but in humility
consider others better than yourselves.
Philippians 2:3

my neighbor. My persistent effort and patience will enable me to find the opportunity that sleeps in every adversity. My character, forged by repeated encounters with adversity, grows stronger and soon becomes capable of accomplishing great things in life.

I will be humble.

Serving my neighbor is one of the greatest acts of humility. Selfish attitudes and behavior can be harmful to my character. I will consider my neighbor's needs before my own. I will be courteous and respectful as I listen to my neighbor's desires and opinions. I am happier when I serve my neighbor with acts of kindness rather than when I seek my own pleasure.

If I find it difficult to keep a humble attitude, I will make it a practice to visit those who are sick or dying. I will not complain or whine when I know there are others who face greater adversity with such dignity.

I will not hesitate to go out of my way or sacrifice my time in order to help a neighbor. To voluntarily suffer for one who is in need of help is one of the greatest acts of unselfish love— whether my neighbor is a friend or stranger.

I will be humble.

I am humble when I practice forgiveness. If I offend my neighbor in any way, I will ask for forgiveness. The act of asking for forgiveness can be one of the most difficult things to do, but those who love their neighbors will humbly ask for it. Since love is a motivating factor in most of my intentions and actions, I am not content until I make peace with my neighbor.

I will be humble in all areas of my life.

- When I tend to boast, I will give credit to others.
- When I receive a compliment, I will say "thank you."
- When I enjoy abundance, I will share it with others.

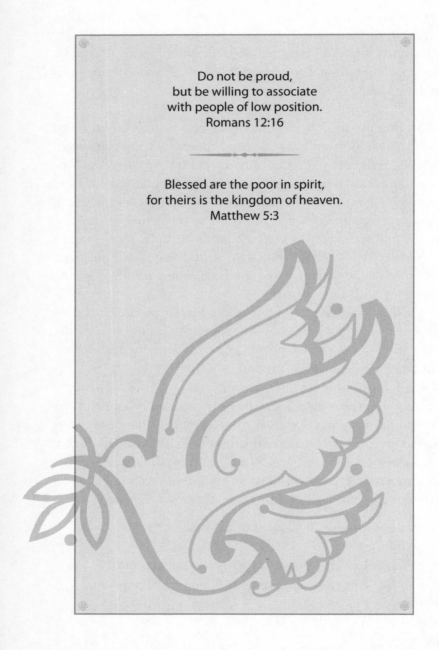

Do not be proud,
but be willing to associate
with people of low position.
Romans 12:16

Blessed are the poor in spirit,
for theirs is the kingdom of heaven.
Matthew 5:3

- When I experience good health, I will help those who are ill.
- When I want to complain or whine, I will help those who are at a disadvantage.
- When I suffer financial hardship, I will increase my service to others.

A humble attitude helps keep me happy with a simple life. It eliminates any desire to concentrate on issues seasoned with vanity, greed, or pride. Humility prevents me from becoming overconfident, careless, or materialistic. With the proper attitude, I'm better equipped to serve my neighbor with love and respect.

A humble child of God realizes that the road of life is bumpy with many obstacles along the way. I need the help of God and neighbor in order to be successful.

The only time I will not face hardships and sorrow is when I pass from this life into eternal life. Therefore, I will make it a practice to humbly kneel before God and ask for patience to bear this life and prepare for the Day of Judgment in hope of attaining eternal life.

CHAPTER 4

FAITHFULNESS

The teacher traveled from one city to another, performing miracles in public places so that everyone could see His great power. He cured the blind, healed the sick, and made the paraplegics walk. The people were so impressed with His great power and wisdom that they followed Him wherever He traveled.

One particular woman had worked her way through the crowd to get close to the teacher. She had suffered painful bleeding for many years; however, she believed that the teacher could heal her. Ashamed and embarrassed, she hid behind others and approached the teacher from behind. With great effort, she struggled to reach in-between people and managed to touch His robe. At that moment, the bleeding stopped for the first time in years, never to return.

The teacher felt His healing power leave Him, so He turned to the woman. The teacher smiled and told her that it was not His robe, but her faith that healed her. He then addressed those around Him . . .

Whatever you ask for in prayer,
believe that you have received it,
and it will be yours.
Mark 11:24

TESTAMENT IV

I WILL HAVE FAITH

Do I believe in the wind when I cannot see it? Do I believe in the sun when the night is dark? Do I believe in my Father when I've never seen His face?

The answers depend on faith. Every person feels the breeze on their skin. Every person sees the morning light as darkness is dispelled. Every person can know the Father though He is invisible.

Faith is the magic ingredient that makes wonderful things possible, even when one doesn't have the means or the know-how. Faith gives us energy, enthusiasm, and hope toward the future. Faith in oneself and faith in God is necessary in order to realize success and happiness.

To have faith is:
- to believe without actually seeing.
- to have confidence in one's ability.
- to demonstrate the determination to succeed.
- to believe in "good" rather than "evil."
- to seek God for help and guidance.
- to hope for eternal life.

I will have faith.

I will have faith in my ability to pursue my dreams and aspirations. Faith allows me to expect good results from my efforts. My thoughts can become a reality only when my determination to succeed is strong enough. My faith in action is an almost unstoppable force.

Because the mind power of two or more people is greater than the mind power of one, I will often choose to work with a group of people. Everyone works as a team when they are dedicated to

I tell you the truth,
he who believes has everlasting life.
I am the bread of life.
John 6:47–48

achieving the same goal. The collective thought power and energy of a group of people working in harmony greatly increases the possibility of the group meeting its objective.

This same principle holds true when I seek God's help and guidance. Great power is created when I work in harmony with God. When I ask God questions and meditate on His answers and His presence in my life, only then will I understand how to think and act in accordance with His will. If my dreams and desires are in accordance with His will, He will help me to be successful and experience great joy.

God's infinite wisdom and inspiration are available for me to call on at any time. Like a good friend, He is always available. Wherever I go, whatever I do, God the Father is always there. What father is not available for the child who needs help?

Without God to guide me, I can become lost or disoriented. If I do not consult God on a regular basis, I am prone to please myself more than I please God or my neighbor. When I aim to please God, I am more likely to think and act in accordance with His will.

My faith in God makes it possible to be cheerful and optimistic about the future. A positive attitude enables me to act with confidence whereas a negative attitude makes it difficult for me to believe in my ability and leads to worry and fear. Because anything is possible with God's help, I can experience wonderful accomplishments when I turn to Him. God's gift of optimism allows me to overcome monumental barriers and scale great mountains. With God's help, I can reach for the stars and dream great dreams.

I will have faith.

By leading a life of faith, I will be prepared for that time when my Father and I meet. My transition from the present life to eternal life is assured when I have faith in God and act in accordance with my faith. I won't complain about my personal unrest—the struggle that is present in my life today. I know

. . . anyone who has faith in me will do
what I have been doing.
John 14:12

that only eternal life is completely free from trouble, adversity, and worry. I know that perfect bliss and union with God await me after I leave this life of faith and hope.

Having faith in God is essential to having faith in me. Because I realize that God is my greatest source of strength and inspiration, I find it easy to have faith in myself. I have great hope in my dreams and goals when I know that God is on my side and is willing to help me.

When I put God first in my life, everything else seems to fall in line. My thoughts, attitudes, and actions are in the proper perspective as I share happiness and joy with those around me. Love and forgiveness enter my heart, as worry and fear seem to vanish.

I believe in myself. I believe in God. I believe in achieving eternal life with God.

CHAPTER 5

MATERIALISM

A few days later, while traveling between cities, a rich, young man came up to the teacher and asked, "Teacher, what must I do to achieve eternal life?" The teacher turned toward the man and told him to sell his possessions and give his money to the poor.

The young man became sad, because he had great wealth. He hung his head, turned, and walked away.

The teacher then spoke to the others . . .

A man's life does not consist
in the abundance of his possessions.
Luke 12:15

TESTAMENT V

I WILL NOT BE MATERIALISTIC

My life is comprised of the spiritual and the material worlds. The spiritual world consists of the mind and spirit. The material world consists of the physical and the tangible. Both are necessary for successful living; however, my primary aim is to concentrate on the spiritual world. To do so, I will not be materialistic.

It is common for people to place too much emphasis on the accumulation and care of material possessions. They devote great portions of time to acquire fancy belongings, elaborate homes, and large sums of money. They become consumed with acquiring bigger and better possessions, not realizing that true comfort comes by owning and maintaining fewer items rather than many.

People who are seriously ill or near death will tell others that the love of family and friends is more important than the love of material things. Because my time on earth is finite, I will not be overly consumed with the care of property or wealth. I prefer that my neighbor is a witness to my acts of goodwill rather than to my objects of achievement. My love of neighbors, friends, and family will always take precedence over the acquiring and maintaining of physical possessions.

- I prefer visiting a neighbor to visiting a vendor.
- I prefer displaying acts of goodwill to displaying items of affluence.
- I prefer earning the trust of a friend to earning a payment or reward.
- I prefer trusting God to trusting society.
- I prefer donating money to charity to donating money to a lottery.

For where your treasure is,
there your heart will be also.
Luke 12:34

- I prefer achieving eternal life to achieving worldly accomplishment.
- I prefer storing treasure in heaven to storing treasure on earth.
- I prefer serving my neighbor with acts of kindness and generosity to serving myself with items of luxury and vanity.

I will not be materialistic.

God created everything, and I realize that everything belongs to Him. Hope, love, and faith are some of God's greatest gifts. Because I am a steward of the Creator's gifts, I will share with others that which He has given me. A smile, a note of thanks, a gift of time, and a word of encouragement are just a few of the things I can share with others. These gifts have far greater value than material gifts that can be lost or stolen.

The act of coveting property will never satisfy me because the focus of this act is on serving myself rather than my neighbor. I am most happy when I serve my neighbor with humble acts of love and compassion. Humble service prevents me from becoming prey to thoughts of greed and envy.

I will serve God, but I cannot serve God and material things. I will replace the love of material and sensuous things with the love of God and neighbor. True happiness and inner security are the result of serving others. I will bow before God and my neighbor, but I will not bow to worldly goods of material comfort.

I will not be materialistic.

I will not yield to conformity. The opinions, attitudes, or actions of an individual or group of individuals may not be in harmony with the laws of God and fellow human beings. Therefore, I will not be overly concerned about public opinion. The approval of family and friends is secondary to God's approval.

Do not worry about your life, what you will eat;
or about your body, what you will wear.
Life is more than food,
and the body more than clothes.
Luke 12:22–23

When I pass from this world, I will not be able to take my belongings with me. Therefore, it does not make sense to spend my time trying to possess more "stuff" than necessary. I am happy with a modest place to live and an ample supply of clothing, along with the means for the necessities of life. Therefore, I will concentrate more on my spiritual life, which brings happiness and peace today as well as tomorrow.

Selfish indulgences (whether sensual or physical), along with worldly influences, can sometimes cause embarrassment and lead to an empty heart. I will make every attempt to concentrate more on the spiritual world by filling my heart with prayer and meditation, prompting me to serve my neighbor with love and respect.

I will not be materialistic.

I will not fall victim to the love of money or property. I will not perform acts of vanity or selfishness. I will not yield to conformity or public opinion. My detachment from material possessions will allow me to have freedom and mobility so that I may better serve God and neighbor. I will lead a life of moderation and purity with acts of kindness and service to others. This is the true path to enlightenment.

CHAPTER 6

THANKSGIVING

The following day, the teacher and a small crowd were traveling between cities when ten men with a skin disease stood at a distance and cried out, "Great teacher, please help us!"

The ten men did not want to come closer to the crowd or the teacher—fearful that their disease might spread among the others.

The teacher told the men to go present themselves to the religious leaders. As soon as they went, their skin disease was healed. One of the ten men, because he had great faith, returned to thank the teacher. The teacher smiled, embraced the grateful man, and addressed the others . . .

Sing and make music in your heart to the Lord,
always giving thanks
to God the Father for everything . . .
Ephesians 5:19–20

TESTAMENT VI

I WILL PRACTICE THANKSGIVING

The greatest gift is the gift of life. I am grateful for the life God has given me, and I'm grateful to share my life with neighbors, friends, and family. My expression of thanksgiving demonstrates my love toward others and helps me to enjoy happy and healthy relationships.

Next to the words, "I love you," the most important words I can say are, "thank you." To say "thank you" means so much but requires very little effort. Giving thanks illustrates my appreciation toward a neighbor's act of kindness and generosity. I will say "thank you" in response to a neighbor's kind action, no matter how large or small the deed may be.

I will practice thanksgiving.

How will I act when a friend sends flowers? How will I act when a neighbor visits me? How will I act when a family member offers me help? Is it best to turn my head and ignore the gesture, or express my appreciation with love and sincerity?

I will seek ways to express my gratitude at every opportunity. My gift of sharing time can go a long way to show my appreciation as well as brighten someone's day. I will share a meal and warm conversation with a friend. I will give a small gift or a note of thanks. I will telephone or pay my neighbor a visit.

When a neighbor expresses thanksgiving in response to my kind words or actions, I can reflect my neighbor's appreciation by replying with a warm, "You're welcome." To say "you're welcome" adds value and sincerity to my gesture. It prevents my actions from appearing fake or insincere.

I will practice thanksgiving.

How will I act when the day greets me with clouds and rain? How will I act when daily living seems too stressful? How will

Devote yourself to prayer,
being watchful and thankful.
Colossians 4:2

I act when plans don't go as hoped? I will act with thanksgiving, for I know that every event happens for a reason and in accordance with God's plan. I must be grateful for every event, good or bad, and learn to find the blessing in every occasion.

I will practice thanksgiving.

Thanksgiving is a means to express love and appreciation toward God. God is the source of every blessing I receive, and I will thank Him at every opportunity.

- I am thankful for the sun and the moon in the heavens.
- I am thankful for the earth and the bounty it provides.
- I am thankful for the trees and the flowers.
- I am thankful for all living creatures.
- I am thankful for the love of neighbor and the support of family and friends.
- I am thankful for the power to choose. If I am not happy with my lot in life, I have the power to choose and create a new field in which to plant my dreams. If I am not happy with my circumstances, I can choose to create new and better circumstances.

Do I appreciate my job and the opportunity it provides? Do I appreciate the meals that I am privileged to eat? Do I appreciate the roof over my head? I will not complain about what I lack, nor will I take each day for granted. I will thank God for the gift of every breath and for His blessings so that I may share them with others.

- If God grants me faith, I will share faith.
- If God grants me hope, I will share hope.
- If God grants me love, I will share love.
- If God grants me grace, I will share grace.

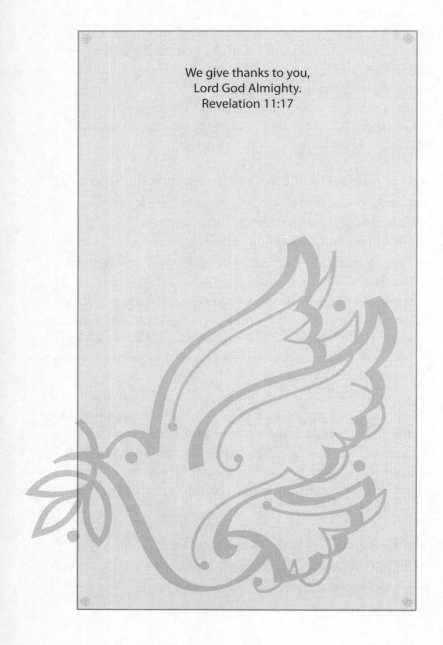

We give thanks to you,
Lord God Almighty.
Revelation 11:17

My humble act of thanksgiving shifts the focus of attention from me, the receiver, to my neighbor, the giver. It prompts me to follow my neighbor's example to become a giver and to serve others. Being thankful expresses my love and praise of God. I will celebrate life with thanksgiving.

CHAPTER 7

SERVICE

O ne evening, the teacher and twelve of His closest friends were gathered when one of the men asked, "How can we better follow you and be more like you?" The teacher filled a basin with water. One by one, He washed their feet and dried them with a towel.

He then stood up and said, "Just as I have washed your feet, you shall wash your neighbor's feet." The men listened closely as the teacher continued . . .

For even the Son of Man did not
come to be served, but to serve . . .
Mark 10:45

TESTAMENT VII

I WILL SERVE MY NEIGHBOR

To love a neighbor is to serve a neighbor. I am truly thankful for everything I have, and I choose to serve others with good and desirable thoughts and actions. Because everyone needs help from time to time, I vow to open my heart and door to any child of God, especially one lacking the means or the necessities of life. I will be likened to the sun by offering rays of hope, and I will spread warmth with acts of generosity, compassion, and understanding.

I will seek to serve others rather than to be served by others. My own needs become secondary when I realize there are many people who need help more than I do. My primary concern is to find a way to provide loving service without expecting recognition or compensation. I will not allow a day to pass without listening to a neighbor's needs and desires, and in some manner assisting a neighbor to a better way of life.

- I will feed the poor.
- I will clothe the naked.
- I will pray with the sinner.
- I will offer encouragement to the downhearted.
- I will provide assistance to the disabled.
- I will find a loving home for the orphaned.
- I will seek refuge for the widowed and exiled.
- I will find justice for those treated unfairly.
- I will pray for the dying.
- I will offer hope for the prisoner.
- I will help the hopeless to have faith.
- I will serve my neighbor.

Share with God's people who are in need.
Practice hospitality.
Romans 12:13

I will assist anyone who lacks the means for the necessities of life. Millions of people in the world need help acquiring food, shelter, and medical assistance. I will volunteer for any organization with a mission to aid others, and it is my hope others will do the same to help or share with a neighbor. A charitable attitude becomes contagious and spreads to other communities.

I will serve my neighbor.

I know that God is the true owner of all money and material possessions. God entrusts me to be a steward of His goods and services by guiding me to give a portion of my income and possessions to others. I will donate items such as furniture, clothes, and other basic necessities to those who do not have the means to acquire such things.

I will serve my neighbor.

If I do not have sufficient money or possessions to give to others, then I can volunteer my time or area of expertise. Anytime I have knowledge on a subject that can benefit others, I will share it. I can write a book, teach a class, or simply read to others who are willing to listen.

I can help my neighbor to become more self-reliant. It is far better to teach a person to fish so he or she may eat for a lifetime than to give someone a fish so he or she may live for a day. It is far better to teach a person to become self-reliant than to allow a person to rely on handouts from society.

There is no task too humble for me to perform.

- I can serve the homeless in a shelter or soup kitchen.
- I can offer transportation to the disabled or volunteer to read to a group of children.
- I can collect coats or sweaters for people who don't have adequate clothing, or play a musical instrument to entertain the elderly or sick in a nursing home.

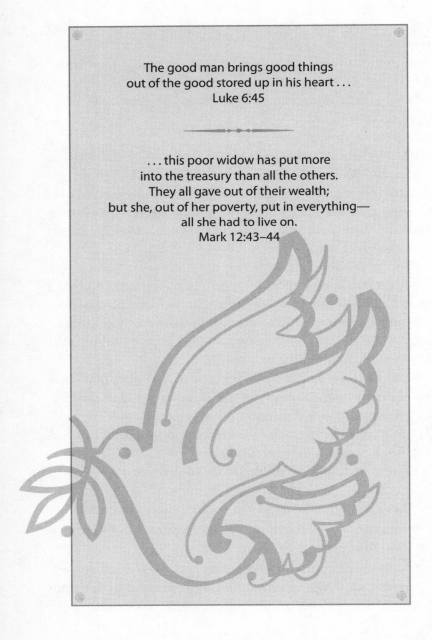

The good man brings good things
out of the good stored up in his heart . . .
Luke 6:45

. . . this poor widow has put more
into the treasury than all the others.
They all gave out of their wealth;
but she, out of her poverty, put in everything—
all she had to live on.
Mark 12:43–44

- I can extend my hand with the simple act of taking the time to listen to people in need of love and support.

Many people, rich or poor, feel unhappy or unfulfilled because they do not know, love, or serve God. True happiness may be discovered in the act of helping others. Participating in recreational activities, resting in leisure, or pursuing a favorite hobby can consume my free time; however, whenever possible, I will engage in helpful actions for a neighbor. It is rewarding to see joy and enthusiasm come to those who feel loved and hopeful about the future.

The act of charity is a way to express love toward my neighbor and God. Giving involves the sacrifice of time and energy, and it brings joy and satisfaction to others in need.

Will I wait for an illness to strike me down? Will I wait for more leisure time? Will I wait for more disposable income? Will I wait for more love to enter my heart? I do not need money or a college degree. All I need is love in my heart, and a little time. The time to begin is today. I may not be here to help my neighbor tomorrow. The time to begin is today.

CHAPTER 8

HONESTY

The great teacher was aware that there were other teachers traveling the countryside, teaching falsely on topics such as wealth, fame, and power. He taught that, just as a tree is known by its fruit, a person is known by his or her deeds.

His followers listened closely when He said to be wary of teachers who do not bear good fruit. He went on to say that a righteous person leads a life of honesty and integrity . . .

In everything set them an example
by doing what is good.
. . . show integrity, seriousness and
soundness of speech that cannot
be condemned . . .
Titus 2:7–8

TESTAMENT VIII

I WILL BE HONEST

My character is the rudder that guides my ship through the ocean of life. The island of failure is the destination for the ship of fools who employ dishonest character, while the shore of happiness awaits those who mold their character with honesty and integrity. I will shape my character with the sound principles of honesty and integrity, with the utmost respect toward my neighbor, God, and all living things.

If my character is forged with honesty and integrity, my neighbor will trust my actions far more than if they are plagued with malice or deceit. It is better to bring happiness and joy to others with actions of integrity than to bring sadness and disappointment with actions of deceit.

My character is formed by my beliefs and actions. Therefore, I will base my beliefs on truth and I will act in accordance with the truth. I will not conform to the beliefs and actions of those who are dishonest. I will follow only those who lead lives based on truth and integrity.

I will be honest.

In the event that a neighbor treats me with dishonest actions, will I react with hatred and anger? Or will I strive for peace with honesty and love? Because I choose to live by the Golden Rule, I will return only thoughts and actions of love and forgiveness. The person who reacts with evil thoughts and actions is likely to burn in the pit of despair, but the person who reacts with kindness will rise to righteousness in the eyes of neighbor and God.

I will not lie, cheat, or steal. Why would I cheat anyone when the same amount of effort is required to be honest and sincere? If I mislead others for personal gain, I waste energy and the opportunity to serve my neighbor in a meaningful way.

Rid yourselves of all malice and
all deceit, hypocrisy, envy,
and slander of every kind.
1 Peter 2:1

God is a witness to my actions, and He knows my every thought and intention. If I mislead my neighbor, I mislead God. If I cheat my neighbor, I cheat God. If I steal from my neighbor, I steal from God. Why should I be deceitful to anyone when I know in my heart that I am also being deceitful to God?

I will be honest.

I will be true to others and myself by adhering to a code of ethics based on honesty and truth. I will take full responsibility for my actions and be fair to everyone with whom I associate. Being true to myself helps me to be true to my neighbor and to God.

I will not cause harm toward a neighbor. Nor will I spread false rumors about my neighbor. I will be sensitive and understanding to the needs of others and show respect with acts of kindness.

I will follow through on my promises and perform the necessary tasks, pleasant or unpleasant, in order to honor my appointments and live up to my responsibilities.

I will obtain permission to borrow a neighbor's possession, and I will return the possession in a timely manner. If I find a neighbor's misplaced possession, I will return it, for I hope my neighbor would do the same for me.

I will be honest.

I will admit my mistakes. To conceal a mistake often leads to further deceit and wrongdoing. Why should I further damage my character and risk injury to a neighbor when it is far easier to admit my mistake and ask for forgiveness?

I will practice good humor. Sharing tasteless jokes or playing pranks can be offensive to others. Why should I risk alienating a neighbor or a potential friend when it is easier to make good humor into a pleasant experience?

I will be loyal to those I am committed to serve. I will be loyal to my spouse. I will be loyal to myself. I will be loyal to God.

The Lord detests lying lips,
but he delights in men who are truthful.
Proverbs 12:22

I will do my best in everything I do, for I know that anything worth doing is worth doing well.

I will not walk in the darkness of evil with immoral or misleading actions. I will make every attempt to eliminate the slightest vice as I strive for only pure and honest thoughts and actions.

The demonstration of high moral standards leads to peace of mind, self-respect, and respect among peers. I will mold my character with the truth and employ the beacon of honesty and integrity to light my path toward peace and prosperity.

CHAPTER 9

ENTHUSIASM

The great teacher told His closest friends that He would not be able to stay with them much longer. Soon the unbelievers would have Him persecuted and put to death.

Saddened, His friends questioned what their mission would be after He left them.

The teacher told them if they continued to believe in Him and proclaim His teachings, even after He was gone, they would acquire a wonderful Spirit, a Spirit that would guide and comfort them . . .

Sing and make music
in your heart to the Lord . . .
Ephesians 5:19

TESTAMENT IX

I WILL BE ENTHUSIASTIC

I have the opportunity to engage the power of enthusiasm by acquiring God's Holy Spirit. The Spirit of God likens me to an oak tree growing strong and tall through the storms of life. The comfort of God's presence gives me the enthusiasm and confidence to forge ahead—resilient to worry and fear. I will embrace the power of the Holy Spirit.

I will be enthusiastic.

I will soar like an eagle high above the clouds of mediocrity as I put forth my best effort in every endeavor. I will not allow a halfhearted endeavor or lack of enthusiasm to spoil my commitment to excellence.

And how will I compose my life? I will allow the presence of God to inspire me to compose my life with energy and enthusiasm like a musician inspired to compose a great symphony. My life will become a dance of excitement and a song of joy when I understand that God's music is within me every step of my journey. I will cherish God's presence in my heart, and I will sing with joy while at work and play.

And how will I act around others? I will act with passion and energy so that those around me will soon glow with the same fire and enthusiasm. I will not be overbearing, boisterous, or fake. I will act in a way that shows respect for my neighbor's feelings, and I will be sensitive to my neighbor's needs and desires. My energy and passion are genuine, and love is foremost in my heart.

I will be enthusiastic.

And how will I motivate myself to be enthusiastic? I will take advantage of adequate rest and leisure and pursue worthwhile goals with faith and energy. A lack of dreams and goals can cause boredom, fatigue, or a lack of excitement. The pursuit

Whatever you do,
work at it with all your heart . . .
Colossians 3:23

of dreams and goals gives me hope, courage, and confident purpose.

How can I make every day extraordinary? With excitement, vitality, and enthusiasm, every day can be extraordinary. I will not employ mundane or lame excuses in order to make it through the day. Why should I go through life accepting mediocre performances or lame excuses? I will concentrate on making every event a wonderful occasion.

I will be enthusiastic.

Pure optimism and passionate enthusiasm make the difference. Those who are optimistic and enthusiastic usually get what they want out of life. They know where they are going and achieve what they want to achieve. They also take the time to help others achieve their dreams. They give their best effort to be optimistic and cheerful in everything they do.

I will be enthusiastic.

I will use enthusiasm to conquer fear and trouble by smiling at the world and laughing at myself. The individual who frowns at the world sees only clouds and rain, but the enthusiastic individual with a sense of humor sees sunshine and rainbows.

What if my enthusiasm begins to wane? Maintaining enthusiasm requires hard work and discipline, and I must remind myself to be cheerful and to smile often. The Spirit of God comes alive in my thoughts and actions when I remind myself that God is always present—the Holy Spirit abides in me and I can concentrate on His presence when my enthusiasm wanes.

Enthusiastic people live in the present moment. There is nothing I can do about yesterday. Yesterday is in the past and I refuse to worry about the past. I realize I might not be here to enjoy tomorrow. I can plan for tomorrow, but I live in the present and enjoy today.

I see the world like a child gazing in wonder and excitement. I will play games, laugh often, and have happy expectations about the future. The world is my playground. I will make

Your eye is the lamp of your body.
When your eyes are good,
your whole body also is full of light.
Luke 11:34

my work enjoyable and exciting. I vow to carry this childlike enthusiasm well into the autumn of my life.

I will use the powerful gift of the Holy Spirit to warm the hearts of people and to guide me through each day. My face will glow with warmth and my eyes will shine with the creative light of enthusiasm.

In the end, my body may be weak and fragile, but my spirit will be alive. My candle will still burn because my spirit commands my being. Eventually, my candle will flicker and my body will fail, but my spirit and soul will live.

I will be creative and unique.

I will be enthusiastic.

CHAPTER 10

OBEDIENCE

The teacher led a large crowd to the top of a hill. He asked the people to bring food and water, and to build fires to keep warm. He planned to meet with them for several days.

That evening, the crowd mingled on the hillside, eating dinner at their leisure. They grew restless, and several people began to question the teacher.

"You have brought us all the way here. What is it you want us to do?" asked a young man.

A woman asked, "How will we know if we are righteous?"

An elderly man asked, "How will we spend the rest of our lives?"

The teacher finished eating His bread and took a sip of water. Then He stood so that everyone could see and hear Him. A quiet calm settled on the hillside as the teacher addressed the crowd . . .

We know that in all things God
works for the good of those who love him,
who have been called according to his purpose.
Romans 8:28

TESTAMENT X

I WILL HEED GOD'S WILL

What is my purpose in life? Does God have a special plan for me? How can I bring goodness to other people? Is my life yielding an abundant harvest, or producing sour grapes? What is God's will for me?

God's will is that I obey the Ten Commandments and the Ten Testaments so that when I pass from this world, I may reside with Him in eternal rest.

I will heed God's will.

I will love my neighbor as myself. I will not judge anyone based on appearance, wealth, race, sex, or religion, nor will I allow the barriers of hatred, greed, or jealousy to hinder my love for my fellow man. I will strive to place my neighbor's interests before my own. To love a neighbor is to love God. I love God most of all, and I vow to spread that love to every family member, friend, and neighbor.

I will practice the two-way street of forgiveness. In the event I am involved in a trespass or misunderstanding with a neighbor, I will do my part to ask or grant forgiveness in order to restore love and trust in the relationship. God has the ultimate power to forgive, and I will ask God for forgiveness and the grace to live in harmony with my neighbor.

I will heed God's will.

I will be humble at all times. I will meet many obstacles and much adversity, and occasionally I will need help from others. I will seek help from my neighbor, and I will humbly kneel before God to ask for divine help. I will not be overconfident, proud, or boastful, but will give credit and thanks to others when due.

I will practice thanksgiving. Because I depend on the help and services of others, I will express my gratitude at every

Not everyone who says to me, 'Lord, Lord,'
will enter the kingdom of heaven,
but only he who does the will of my Father
who is in heaven.
Matthew 7:21

opportunity. When I awake each morning, I will thank God for the blessing to untie the ribbon of a new day, and for the serendipity to discover the treasures hidden in everyday tasks.

I will not be materialistic. I will not allow the material world to hinder my spiritual progress or diminish time enjoyed with loved ones. My love for God, family, and friends will always take precedence over the acquiring and maintaining of physical possessions. Because I replace the love of material and sensuous things with the love of God, family, and friends, I am free to love and serve God and His people.

I will serve my neighbor. I will find ways to provide loving service to others. Because God is the true owner of all money and possessions, He entrusts me to give a portion of my income and possessions to those who lack the means for the necessities of life. I can also volunteer my time and knowledge to those who may benefit.

I will employ honesty and integrity as my guides. I will not walk in the darkness of evil with immoral or deceitful actions. I am determined to choose the "right thing," and I will allow the beacon of honesty and integrity to light my path to peace and prosperity.

I will be enthusiastic. God's presence in my life gives me enthusiasm and a resiliency to worry and fear. With the Spirit of God, I will soar like an eagle high above the clouds of mediocrity as I pursue a clear vision with confidence. I will put forth my best effort with an enthusiastic passion and a commitment to excellence.

I will have faith. Faith is the magic ingredient that gives me energy and hope for the future. Faith in God helps me have faith in others and myself. Great power is created when I have faith in the Almighty. When I ask the Father questions and meditate on His answers and His presence in my life, only then do I understand how to think and act in accordance with God's

For my Father's will is that everyone who
looks to the Son and believes in him
shall have eternal life,
and I will raise him up at the last day.
John 6:40

will. If my dreams and desires are in accordance with His will, He will help me be successful and to experience great joy.

God helps me discover His will by sometimes sending adversity and struggle. I may not fully understand why certain things happen, but when I live by these Ten Testaments, my life becomes one of purpose and direction. I understand that God loves me and wants me to reside with Him after leading a fruitful life of loving service to others.

THE TEN TESTAMENTS PRAYER

Lord, thank You for bestowing upon me Your
unending love and grace.
Free my mind from all worries and selfish pursuits.
Guide me to love and serve my neighbor with
honesty and integrity.
Allow me to maintain peace and harmony
with my neighbor and
grant me the power of forgiveness in times of conflict.
Keep me humble so I may seek treasure in heaven,
not treasure on earth, and
grant me the faith to pursue Your will with
passion and enthusiasm.
Amen.

ENDNOTES

This book is intended to summarize and clarify the teachings of Jesus. It is not meant to substitute or replace the Gospel of Jesus. For a more in-depth understanding of Jesus' message and teachings, please refer to The New Testament of the Holy Bible.

For more information about the author, *The Ten Testaments Study Guide, The Ten Testaments Audio Book* and other programs including group purchase quantity discounts, please visit: www.thetentestaments.com